Margaret Bourke-White

Margaret Bourke-White

RACING WITH A DREAM

CATHERINE A. WELCH

CAROLRHODA BOOKS, INC./MINNEAPOLIS

00 June s
Lerner
2393(179?)

To Rose Lee and Diane

The author wishes to thank Ingrid Davis, Cynthia Baklik, and the staff of the Monroe (Connecticut) Public Library for their help in gathering material for this book.

The publisher wishes to thank Carolyn Davis and staff at the George Arents Research Library for Special Collections at Syracuse University, Syracuse, New York.

Carolrhoda Books, Inc., c/o The Lerner Publishing Group
241 First Avenue North, Minneapolis, MN 55401 U.S.A.

Website address: www.lernerbooks.com

Library of Congress Cataloging-in-Publication Data

Welch, Catherine A.
  Margaret Bourke-White : racing with a dream / by Catherine A. Welch.
      p. cm.
    Includes bibliographical references and index.
    Summary: Examines the personal life and photographic career of the woman who served as a photojournalist for the magazine "Life" during World War II and the Korean War.
    ISBN 1-57505-049-8 (alk. paper)
    1. Bourke-White, Margaret, 1904–1971—Juvenile literature.
  2. News photographers—United States—Biography—Juvenile literature. 3. Women photographers—United States—Biography—Juvenile literature. [1. Bourke-White, Margaret, 1904–1971.
  2. Women photographers. 3. Photographers. 4. Women—Biography.]
  I. Title.
  TR140.B6W46   1998
  770'.92—dc21
  [b]   97-37939

Manufactured in the United States of America
1 2 3 4 5 6 – JR – 03 02 01 00 99 98

Contents

Foreword

"It is harder for a woman than a man to start something," said Margaret Bourke-White, "but once she gets started she has an easier time because her accomplishments attract more attention than a man's would."

In the early 1900's, when Margaret grew up, it was not easy for a woman to start something—something more challenging than handling a yeast dough or tilling a garden bed. Men were the doers of bold deeds. Men were the pioneers. Men were the history-makers.

In the field of photography, some women had established themselves with profitable careers. But few dared to probe the exciting or tragic events of their time. Gertrude Stanton Kasebier was known for her portrait work. Frances Benjamin Johnston made portraits, photographed workers in mines and factories, and took photos of homes and other buildings, including the White House. May Jobe Akeley—an explorer and photographer—worked in Africa, photographing animals and their surroundings.

But Margaret, determined to have a life of thrilling adventure, embraced photography on a grand scale. With a child's curiosity, an artist's eye, and an explorer's spirit, Margaret became known as the daring girl with a camera.

At a time when developments in camera and printing processes thrust photography into the limelight, Margaret became one of the most famous photographers not only in this country, but throughout the world.

Margaret White was born June 14, 1904 (at Harrison Avenue in the Bronx, New York City) to parents who planned to set no boundaries on her life.

Margaret's mother, Minnie Bourke White, was the daughter of an Irish ship's carpenter and an English cook. Joseph, her father, was the son of Polish Jews. Independent people, both dared to break from their families' traditions and lifestyles. Minnie was spirited and eager to learn, unlike the rest of her less ambitious family. Joseph, a man who disliked displays of affection, rejected his family's Orthodox Jewish traditions, and devoted his life to work. According to Minnie's cousin, they were not married in a church or synagogue, but by an atheist minister. (An atheist is a person who doesn't believe in God.).

Together, Minnie and Joseph raised Margaret and her older sister, Ruth, and younger brother, Roger, with a serious approach to life. They encouraged their children to do their best and become independent. From the start, Margaret was destined to be different and do great things.

1
Dreams and Fears

Eight-year-old Margaret followed her father, Joseph, into the factory. She did not know what would happen. But the building's hissing and shuddering machines spoke of adventure and promised that the afternoon would not be a disappointment. Silently Margaret followed Joseph up a metal stairway to a sooty iron balcony and stared into the blackness below them. "Wait," said her father. Margaret waited.

Then suddenly, Margaret was surprised by a fiery flow of light beneath them. Thrilled, Margaret watched in amazement at the glowing hot metal and flying sparks.

Margaret lived for moments like this. Moments of drama, beauty, and the unexpected. As a child, she searched for excitement and was eager to learn new things. Quick to spot a challenge, Margaret invited adventure into her daily routine. Even a walk to school became a daring test of skill, as she and her sister, Ruth, did a balancing act across the top of wooden fences.

Margaret *(second from left)* with her brother, Roger *(far left),* her sister, Ruth *(standing),* and her mother, Minnie *(far right).*

Challenges also came from her father during their nature walks in the woods near their Bound Brook, New Jersey home. There, Joseph encouraged Margaret to handle the snakes that slithered across their path. He taught Margaret how to recognize the harmless ones, and showed her how to pick them up without being afraid.

Margaret was the perfect subject for her father's lessons. Soon she began bringing snakes home. Snakes became favorite pets, especially when Margaret realized the attention she could command from her classmates by bringing the snakes to the four-room schoolhouse. Though harmless, they could put on a startling show, particularly her puff adder, which inflated its neck and let out threatening hisses. It was a frightening display for the children, and Margaret delighted in every moment. She enjoyed *doing* the unexpected as much as she *enjoyed* the unexpected.

In fact, in her daydreams, Margaret saw herself "doing all the things that women never do." She dreamed of becoming a herpetologist (a scientist who studies reptiles and amphibians) and traveling to the jungle. She saw herself becoming an expert in the field and being sent on important expeditions.

As a small child, Margaret found the idea of traveling so powerful that she frequently ran away from home. She didn't get far, though. Her mother usually found her after she'd gone one or two blocks. Later on, Margaret satisfied her desire to roam in other ways. In the winter, she and Ruth skated the ten-mile frozen trail of the drained Raritan Canal.

At home, Minnie did her part to nurture her daughter's curiosity. She made an adventure of learning. The Whites' stucco house became a haven for all sorts of creatures, and the walls were decorated with maps. Along with the snakes, there were turtles, rabbits, and hamsters. One summer, Margaret studied and cared for two hundred caterpillars, which she kept under rows of overturned glasses on the dining room windowsill.

Even as a baby, Margaret loved to be in nature, where she could discover new things.

Margaret's parents demanded a great deal of their children. Margaret and Ruth took music lessons, received sewing and cooking lessons from Minnie, and attended concerts. The White children were expected to pour every ounce of themselves into a task. Margaret wrote in her autobiography, "If my sister or I took one of those school examinations where you are required to answer only ten questions out of twelve, Mother's comment on hearing this would be, 'I hope you chose the ten hardest ones.' Reject the easy path! Do it the hard way!"

Minnie's standards were so high that Ruth and Roger found her criticism difficult to bear at times. But Margaret, with boundless energy to match her mother's, seemed to thrive on Minnie's demand for perfection—even when perfection meant facing her fears.

Both Minnie and Joseph emphasized the importance of courage. While Joseph made his contribution with the snakes, Minnie used fiery words and clever games. "Go right up and look your fears in the face," she instructed Margaret, "and then *do* something!"

One by one, Margaret faced her problems, such as her fears of the dark and staying alone in the house. On moonlit nights, she followed Minnie outside. She raced her mother around the house, and soon discovered that the darkness was something to enjoy and not fear. Other nights, Margaret tried staying in the house alone. At first, her parents left her alone for only a few minutes. Margaret passed the time by reading a favorite book or doing a jigsaw puzzle. After a while, Margaret was able to stay alone for hours and enjoy the time by herself.

Joseph White, Margaret's father, was a moody man, but Margaret still adored him.

Each day in the Whites' house shone with accomplishment. Yet at times, this light was dimmed by Margaret's father. Joseph White was an inventor who spent much of his time thinking about ways to improve printing presses. Margaret and the other children were not allowed to disturb him when he was "thinking." Life revolved around a moody man who spent hours thinking in his easy chair or stooped over his drawing board. Joseph seldom talked to his children.

Minnie Bourke White, Margaret's mother, had boundless energy. She was able to encourage her children's curiosity by making learning fun and interesting.

Minnie considered her husband's silence an unbearable flaw in his character. But Margaret overlooked it as much as she could and adored her father. The times she spent with him were special. When Joseph became interested in the camera, Margaret thought it was an exciting treat when she and the other children were used as subjects for his many photographs. And though Minnie suffered, Margaret saw only her mother's willingness to help Joseph.

Often, Margaret saw her father bolt from the dinner table, suddenly stricken with an idea which needed to be put down into words. She saw her mother chase after him ready to record his thoughts on paper. Their devotion to work, like a steady flame, kindled a lasting message in Margaret's mind—work is everything!

While Joseph's silence did not trouble Margaret, Minnie's strict rules did. Forbidden to chew gum, wear silk stockings, or play cards, Margaret felt the pain of being left out as she watched other children doing these things. The White children were not allowed to go to the movies with any frequency or read the funny papers (as the comics were called). They couldn't even play in homes where there were funny papers, because Minnie thought it would harm their artistic development. Margaret, a plain, shy little girl, with "long hair parted in the middle and pulled back into pigtails," missed being part of her friends' antics.

In high school, at Plainfield High in New Jersey, Margaret loved to dance and longed for boys to ask her to dances, but no one did. Being noticed wasn't the problem. Boys asked her to picnics and canoe trips, and Margaret attracted a great deal of attention in high school. By her senior year, she was involved in the debate club and the senior play, and was editor of the yearbook and president of the Dramatic Club. In Margaret's eyes, the problem was her mother's too-strict rules. But Minnie's rules were only part of the problem. Margaret, with her broad jaw, looked serious. Margaret, with her pet snakes and grand ambitions, was different.

2

A New Curiosity

In the fall of 1921, Margaret started Columbia University hoping to shed the plain, shy-girl image. She wanted to belong, and she wanted men to find her attractive. That first year, the dates did come and so did the dances. Though still clinging to her ambitions, Margaret began to see and believe that she was attractive.

Unfortunately, her early college days were shattered by a heartbreaking event. In January 1922, Joseph White died, leaving Margaret grieving—and scrambling for the next semester's tuition. Joseph was a talented inventor, but his impressive "thinking" did not extend to money matters. The father Margaret adored left his family with little. For a while, it looked like Margaret would not be able to return to college. Then Margaret's Uncle Lazar, Joseph's brother, offered to help with tuition, and Margaret was able to continue her studies.

In 1921 Margaret left New Jersey for New York City to start college at Columbia University.

When Margaret returned to school, she found a way of keeping her father's memory alive. She decided to take a course in photography, which had been Joseph's hobby. This new interest in photography did not mean Margaret had abandoned herpetology or her dream of trekking to the jungle. It had occurred to Margaret that having photographic skills might be useful to a scientist. After all, someone had to visually document life in the wild.

As always, Minnie encouraged her daughter's new curiosity. Somehow she found twenty dollars to spare and bought Margaret a secondhand camera, an old Ica Reflex with a cracked lens.

The course Margaret took was with Clarence H. White, a short, gentle man, and a well-known photographer who believed that photography was an art. From him, Margaret learned the elements of design and composition—

how close to stand from the subject; where to position the camera in terms of the subject (left, right, up, or down). She also learned the soft-focus technique which gave photographs a blurry, painting-like quality. Margaret enjoyed the work, and at the end of freshman year, she took her new skills and applied for a summer job teaching photography to children at Camp Agaming on Lake Bantam, Connecticut.

At the camp, Margaret taught with an assistant, Madge Jacobson, who helped develop the film. In addition, Margaret filled in as the nature counselor. Her interest and background with crawling and fluttering creatures made her a natural at entertaining the lively campers.

At eighteen, Margaret had the patience and determination of an experienced photographer. She stayed up all night with her camera so she could catch the sunrise at Lake Bantam. She hiked up mountains and thought nothing of taking a dangerous stance on the top to capture the breathtaking view.

Quick to spot a money-making opportunity, Margaret also started a business, selling postcards of the camp, the campers, and their bunks. She worked long hours in the darkroom and learned how to enlist others to help. Margaret told stories to amuse her two child volunteers and rewarded Madge with a camera at the end of the summer.

Printing almost two thousand cards gave Margaret great satisfaction, and she began to see herself as someone capable of earning a living. But while the money Margaret made helped, it wasn't enough for her second year at college. Once again, it looked as if Margaret would not be able to continue her education. Then some generous and well-to-do people in the neighborhood took an interest in Margaret. Mr. Munger and his sister (both unmarried) heard about Margaret's talent and her financial problem. The Mungers, who had supported several young people through college, decided to help Margaret. They gave Margaret money for tuition and clothes, and directed her to get the most out of college, including a social life.

Margaret's self-confidence soared as a result of the Mungers' gift. (Not many people have a stranger offer to support them through college!) Margaret entered the University of Michigan, still intent on studying herpetology but equipped with a new outlook. In the daytime, she still wrapped herself in a cheerless look, but she escaped in the evening with "fancy clothes" for dances.

Margaret liked to get dressed up for evening parties during her college years.

Of course, Margaret still led her life just a little differently from other women. She brought a pet snake for her room, and on dates she sometimes asked the men to take her to the railroad station to watch the engines.

At Michigan, Margaret's interest in photography continued. After impressing the editor with her soft-focus photos, she began working for the student yearbook, the *Michiganensian* (usually called the *'Ensian*).

For a while, Joe Vlack, another photographer for the *'Ensian,* was attracted to her. Anxious to spend time with Margaret, Vlack kept her interest by leading her and her camera on campus adventures. Together they photographed the clock tower from a window in a men's bathroom on the fourth floor. For other shots, they climbed up a rope to a rooftop and crawled down a manhole ladder to a dark tunnel.

While studying at the University of Michigan, Margaret took pictures of many different campus buildings, like this one.

Margaret found these moments of adventure exciting, and soon they were directing her away from herpetology. She wondered if there might be a world of photographic thrills waiting for her reckless spirit. She told Dr. Alexander G. Ruthven, the university zoologist, that she wanted to write—perhaps to be a photographer-reporter. Dr. Ruthven also felt that herpetology might not be her calling, although at one point he suggested that she might like to write and take photographs for nature stories. He sensed she was a person with the potential for great achievement, destined to do something on a colossal scale, but biology did not seem to be it.

While sorting this out, Margaret fell in love with a graduate electrical engineering student, Everett Chapman. In Margaret's words, "Chappie was six feet tall with the shoulders of a football player [and] black snapping eyes." He was fun, like her father had sometimes been, and at nineteen, she planned to marry him.

But before Margaret could marry Chappie, she had to deal with an inner conflict—one that drove her to a psychiatrist. Margaret struggled with feelings of not belonging and of being inferior to others. She also struggled with the secret of the fact that her father was Jewish.

Although religion was not a big part of the White household, Margaret knew of her Christian heritage and sometimes went to church. But as a child, Margaret did not even know that her father was Jewish. Joseph did not think of himself as a Jew, Minnie had no fondness for Jews, and the White children rarely saw their father's relatives. During this time of great anti-Semitism (prejudice against Jews) in America, Margaret did not want any connection with her Jewish heritage.

As it turned out, though, Margaret's tie to Judaism was not an obstacle for Chappie, as she had feared it would be. They were married on June 13, 1924. Their marriage was doomed to failure from the first day, however, by an obstacle more destructive than Margaret's secret. The obstacle was Chappie's mother.

While Minnie White was concerned that Margaret had not yet finished college, she wished the young couple well. Mrs. Chapman, on the other hand, viewed the marriage of her son as his death. She could not accept the fact that her son was leaving her and getting married. At the ceremony, she cried, loudly and mournfully, as if she were at a funeral. She made sure she injected a powerful dose of bad feelings into the marriage.

Everett Chapman had mood swings similar to Margaret's father's. When Chappie became silent and unapproachable, Margaret felt lonely and sad.

Margaret and her new husband tried to make a go of their marriage. They moved to Purdue University (in Indiana) for a year. There Chappie taught, and Margaret studied paleontology—prehistoric life forms (plant and animal fossils). Then in 1925, Chappie took a job with the Lincoln Electric Company, and they moved to Cleveland. During this second year of their marriage, Margaret worked in the Museum of Natural History teaching public school children. At night she attended the Case Western Reserve School, majoring in education.

Those two years of marriage were a miserable and lonely time for Margaret. Though she had adored an often silent father, she found Chappie's frequent silent moods unbearable. After two years, the marriage ended.

Margaret was relieved to be out of the marriage. She was happy to have her independence back and accepted the failure of her marriage as a kind of gift. In her autobiography, she wrote, "I owe a peculiar debt to my mother-in-law. She left me strong, knowing I could deal with a difficult experience, learning from it, and leaving it behind without bitterness, in a neat closed room."

With the shambles of a stormy marriage behind Margaret, the winds of work blew again. She made plans to finish her studies at Cornell in Ithaca, NY. "I chose Cornell," she later wrote, "not for its excellent zoology courses but because I read there were waterfalls on the campus."

Cornell's scenic campus supplied Margaret with an opportunity to earn money by establishing a photography business once again. With her old Ica Reflex in hand, she took pictures at dawn through layers of mist. On winter nights, she captured the beauty of buildings encircled in snow. At times, she climbed "all over the ice around the [frozen] waterfalls," which through her eyes looked "like great organ pipes." Still using the soft-focus effect, Margaret worked long hours in the darkroom so her photos would have a blurry, painting-like quality.

Her dramatic photos were a hit. Margaret had so much business that she hired student workers to help sell her photos. Though her business was an overall suc–cess, Margaret had one problem. When she saw that the photographs were selling, she invested time and money into printing large quantities of the photos. Then, sud-denly, sales stopped. It was months before sales picked up again.

Time passed, and Margaret continued to invest more time in photography than in her nature studies. She took a course in journalism and submitted a photograph to the *Cornell Alumni News,* which later began paying her five dollars on a regular basis for photographs of the campus buildings.

The attention did not stop there. Several Cornell alumni (graduates) who were architects sent her letters. They were impressed with her work and wondered if she planned to be an architectural photographer after gradua-tion. Margaret seemed to see buildings differently than other photographers. To her, buildings were more than stone structures. With her camera, Margaret was able to capture the character of a building. The Cornell alumni made it sound like Margaret would do well in the field.

During Margaret's studies at Cornell, she worked to perfect her soft-focus-effect photography. Her hard work paid off—her photos were a great success.

Though the letters bolstered Margaret's confidence, and made her seriously consider photography as a career, she was unsure of how seriously to take them. She knew the alumni had a sentimental attachment to Cornell. When these people viewed her photographs of the campus buildings, fond memories of their college days may have clouded their judgment. Before she could abandon her dreams of jungle adventures, she had to be sure of her photographic abilities—especially since it looked like she might be offered a job by the curator of herpetology at the Museum of Natural History in New York.

In an effort to settle the question of her future, Margaret took her pictures to York & Sawyer, a large architectural firm in New York. When she was assured that she could "walk into any architect's office in the country with [her] portfolio and get work," she made a decision. Photography would be her life's work.

3

Beauty in the Mills

Margaret began her photographic journey in Cleveland, Ohio. She began using her full name, Margaret Bourke-White, adding a hyphen between her middle and last names. (Her mother had chosen Bourke for Margaret's middle name, hoping she would use it.) It was 1927, a time when the country's eye was on industry. With her love of machines, Margaret found it easy to fall in step with the country's fascination with technology.

Margaret thrived on the "nervous life" of Cleveland. She roamed the city of soaring office buildings, exhilarated by the sights and sounds. Her desire to work was strengthened by the power and motion of the chugging locomotives, roaring traffic, and tugboats pushing barges on the Cuyahoga River.

In Cleveland, Ohio, Margaret photographed many of the city's sites, including this one of the Terminal Tower.

In her spare time, Margaret explored the factory districts snapping pictures of smokestacks, bridges, and water tanks. She became a part of the industrial world and the modern age—constantly on the go, always looking for new and improved ways of doing things. She began seeing the camera as a vehicle for showing the truth. She had started to abandon the soft-focus technique at Cornell, and in Cleveland she completely changed her style. Her photos were now in sharp focus, showing the textures of her subjects, with their every line and graceful curve.

Though few women had photographed industrial subjects up till that time, Margaret was just the woman to compete with the men in this field. But the pictures she took in her spare time, of smokestacks and bridges, were not paying her bills. So she took samples of her work to architects and landscapers, hoping they would hire her to photograph the buildings and estate gardens they designed.

She approached her potential clients with wide-eyed enthusiasm and a bundle of recommendations from architects who knew her work. And if she thought a dazzling smile would help, she turned on the charm. Margaret paid attention to every detail of her presentation, including her clothing.

At the time, her business wardrobe consisted of one gray suit and two sets of hats and gloves—one blue, the other red. When she met her clients, she recorded what she wore. If she wore the blue hat and gloves the first time, at the second meeting she wore the red hat and matching gloves.

After leaving Cornell, Margaret changed her photographic style. She stopped taking pictures in soft-focus and began to take photos in sharp focus.

Her efforts paid off within a short period of time. Margaret secured her first job in the city, working for two Cornell-trained architects, Mr. Mott and Mr. Pitkin. They needed a photo of a school they had designed to submit to *Architecture* magazine. One photographer had tried to produce an acceptable photo but failed.

The assignment presented a challenge for Margaret, as the school was surrounded by construction debris. But for Margaret, who always welcomed a challenge, it was a problem with a solution. She bought "an armful of asters [and] stuck them in the muddy ground." Then she took pictures from a ground position. She aimed the camera over the tops of the flowers, which made it seem as if the plants were part of the scenery. Mott and Pitkin were delighted with the results. The pictures were published, and Margaret received more work from the firm and from others.

It wasn't long before she founded the Bourke-White Studio. The studio—her one-bedroom apartment with a "stack of developing trays in the kitchen sink" and a hide-a-bed in the living room—wasn't lavish. But Margaret made do. She greeted her clients in the living room and used the kitchenette and bathtub to develop her prints.

Along the way, Margaret became friends with a camera-store clerk, Alfred Hall Bemis, whom she called Beme. He gave her technical pointers and encouraged her to set aside time to eat properly. He also gave her some good advice. When Margaret began worrying about the competition, he told her, "Don't worry about what the other fellow is doing. Shoot off your own guns."

Margaret took photos of people's homes and gardens for architect clients, like this photo of the Briggs's estate, while working in Cleveland during the 1920s.

While working for architects and landscape designers, Margaret thought about how she could "shoot off her own guns." These jobs paid the bills, but they were not satisfying, particularly since she longed to enter the industrial world. For Margaret, stately buildings and peaceful gardens could not compare with the action of powerful machinery and its fiery products.

In an effort to break into this field, Margaret followed a friend's suggestion and took a portfolio of her work to one of Cleveland's banks. As a result, she began doing covers for the bank's monthly magazine, *Trade Winds,* earning an additional fifty dollars a month. With this extra income, Margaret was able to put a down payment on a used car. She was also able to add "a third color to her wardrobe—purple," by sewing a dress herself.

But this was only a beginning. Margaret had her mind set on photographing the inside of the steel mills. While others looked at the outside of these buildings and saw ugliness, Margaret looked toward the inside, where she saw beauty and excitement.

The door to the steel mills was not readily opened for women, however. The mills were a dangerous place—a place of intense heat and acid fumes. Margaret was told that twenty years earlier a schoolteacher visiting a mill had fainted. But Margaret—who was sure she would not faint—kept talking to people. Eventually she was able to meet with Elroy Kulas, president of Otis Steel.

At their meeting, Mr. Kulas sat behind his desk. Margaret approached with courage and enthusiasm. She told him how she felt that inside the mills there was a "hidden beauty that was waiting to be discovered. And recorded!"

Mr. Kulas listened patiently to Margaret. He studied her pictures. He thought her photos of flower gardens were lovely. But he didn't believe Margaret could find anything artistic in the steel mills and didn't think she'd have any worthwhile photos to purchase. Nevertheless, Margaret's forceful pleading persuaded him to give her permission to enter the mills and use her camera.

While Kulas headed off to Europe for five months, Margaret went into the steel mills almost every night that winter. She used the money she got from her day jobs to pay for the film. The first night, she entered the mill dressed in a "flimsy skirt and high-heeled slippers." She didn't know what to shoot or what to do. Lighting was the biggest problem. Some parts of the mill were very bright because of the furnaces. But other parts were dark. Yet when she stood among the "riot of flying sparks, rushing metal, [and] bursts of smoke," she felt at home.

Her friend Beme went with her that first night and never forgot her excitement. Years later he told Margaret, "You were dancing on the edge of the fiery crater in your velvet slippers, taking pictures like blazes and singing for joy."

But the night manager was not singing for joy. He thought Margaret was a nuisance because she distracted the men, and he worried about her safety. Margaret didn't care what he thought. She was more concerned with her photos.

The first pictures came out badly. Since the mill was so dark, the film was not exposed to much light. There wasn't much detail in Margaret's pictures. For weeks, Margaret borrowed supplies from Bemis and experimented with floodlights and flashpans. But nothing seemed to work.

Margaret preferred to take striking industrial photos, like this one, rather than pictures of stately buildings.

Just as things began to look hopeless, help came from an unexpected source—a traveling salesman named H. F. Jackson, whom Bemis had known as a teenager. Jackson had twelve large flares that he hoped could be used in Hollywood movies. Like Bemis, it wasn't long before he got caught up in Margaret's enthusiasm. He decided to let Margaret use eleven flares and saved only one to demonstrate in Hollywood.

While Bemis and Jackson held the flares, Margaret took several pictures. And the flares did the trick. The developed prints showed everything: ladles, giant hooks and cranes, even the path of sparks splashing from the flowing hot metal.

Other photographers had taken photos of the steel mills, but their pictures were lifeless. Margaret's were alive with the drama and magic of things under construction, things in motion, things glowing.

When Kulas returned from Europe, he bought eight of the prints at $100 each and ordered an additional eight. He used them in a book called *The Story of Steel,* which he sent to his stockholders. Margaret's industrial photographs soon caught the country's attention.

4

Drama on the Assembly Line

As Margaret focused her camera on industry, she quickly earned a reputation as a bold and daring young woman, and the press was beginning to follow her story. On April 25, 1929, only two years into her career, the *New York Sun* ran the following headline: "DIZZY HEIGHTS HAVE NO TERRORS FOR THIS GIRL PHOTOGRAPHER, WHO BRAVES NUMEROUS PERILS TO FILM THE BEAUTY OF IRON AND STEEL." Margaret enjoyed the attention and recognized that this publicity could be the edge she needed to make it in a man's world. It certainly didn't hurt.

In July 1929, magazine publisher Henry R. Luce decided to put out a new magazine called *Fortune*. He intended the magazine for businessmen and wanted to explore every aspect of business and industry—factories and their machines, tractors and railroads. But Luce also wanted the magazine to be beautiful. After seeing Margaret's photographs of the steel mills, Luce flew Margaret to New York for an interview, and she was chosen as a photographer for the first issue.

Until this time, words had had the spotlight in magazines. But Luce was about to change that. With *Fortune,* pictures were to become equal partners with words. Articles were to have dramatic pictures—pictures he was sure Margaret could deliver. "The camera," Margaret later recalled Luce saying, "should explore every corner of industry, showing everything."

Probing dusty corners became Margaret's specialty. For the first issue of *Fortune,* she spent a week exploring the Swift meat-packing plant in Chicago. Together with Parker Lloyd-Smith, a young editor, Margaret examined every aspect of the operation for the magazine's first article, "Hogs."

Henry Luce started a new magazine called *Fortune* in 1929.

Margaret explored all aspects of the meat industry in a meat-packing plant in Chicago. Her work appeared in "Hogs," which marked the beginning of photographic essays.

Slaughter on the assembly line! Margaret's camera caught everything—the rear ends of live pigs, the bodies of dead pigs hanging in rows, people trimming, cutting, and packaging the finished hams. Margaret even braved the final storeroom, where scraps of bone and flesh were turned to "pig dust." Death's reeking odor sent Lloyd-Smith running to the car, but Margaret toughed it out and took her photographs.

"Hogs" was an important step in photojournalism, or news photography, and for Margaret's career. It was a beginning move toward what is now known as the photographic essay, as her pictures told a story.

Margaret went to great lengths—sometimes putting herself in danger—to get spectacular pictures.

For the next several years, Margaret worked six months of each year for *Fortune* and the other six for advertising agencies. By 1931 she was living in New York City, in an expensive studio on the sixty-first floor of the Chrysler Building, with a large terrace for parties, a small terrace for two pet alligators, and a pair of stainless steel gargoyles outside her window. The gargoyles hung eight hundred feet over the street and cried out for her attention. Margaret could not resist crawling out on them and taking pictures of the city.

Margaret spent part of her time working on advertising accounts—particularly automobile—while employed with *Fortune*. Assisted by Eddie Rickenbacker, she set up a photo at the Indianapolis Speedway.

Her advertising accounts paid well, particularly the ones for Buick cars and Goodyear tires. But while the money was good, she felt that commercial work restricted her as an artist. To satisfy her clients, she had to see things from an advertiser's point of view instead of her own, which was often unsettling for Margaret.

Years later Margaret said in an interview, "Here, for example, is the automobile—shining and showy—with the smiling models bound for the skating rink and ski jumps. My trouble is that I see the automobile in many other spots—plowing in a rainstorm, suffering from a blowout, running out of gas." When Margaret's time with *Fortune* rolled around each year, she was relieved.

One of her early *Fortune* assignments, in 1930, sent her to Germany to examine the leading industries in that country. And after that, it was on to Russia. She had heard a lot of talk about Russia and their Five Year

Plan—the plan to industrialize their country almost overnight. Margaret was curious. "I had been in factories enough to appreciate that industry has a history," she wrote, "machines are developed and men grow along with them." Margaret wondered how the Russian peasants—who knew only the plow—would manage with the new machines. She felt this was an important event and wanted to record it.

Though the editors at *Fortune* were also interested in Russia, they did not think Margaret would be able to get permission to photograph that country's industries. At the time, photographers from foreign countries were not welcome in Russia. But Margaret was not discouraged. Her love for machines—and for the challenge of being first—made her more determined. She applied for a Russian visa, which she received a few months later with the help of her portfolio of industrial pictures.

At the same time, she received a warning from an American journalist. "You must buy a cheap trunk and fill it with canned food," said the American reporter. "That is not advice. It is an order!" Margaret had heard that getting food in Russia could be an ordeal. Food production there was low. People often had to wait in line all day to get what little was available. Not wanting to risk getting sick, she bought a trunk and filled it with cheese, chocolate, canned fruit, and baked beans.

Once in Russia, Margaret waited only two days before she was granted permission to photograph. Her Cleveland portfolio quickly won over the authorities. The Russians thought the machine would save them—put more

In Russia, Margaret began to take more pictures that featured people.

food on their tables and bring them better living conditions. The drama and beauty of Margaret's photos spoke to the Russians in a way they understood. They became convinced her photos would not harm but rather would boost the morale of the country in achieving its goal. In fact, they decided that Margaret was to be a guest of the government with all expenses paid.

But there were more delays. The Russian railroad experts had to hold conferences, study the maps, check the train schedule. It was a while before she and her interpreter finally set off.

When they did, their days were a whirlwind of activity. First Margaret saw the dam under construction in Dnieperstroi, then the collective farms in Rostov, and the cement factory in the seaport of Novorossisk. In

Stalingrad she toured a steel plant that was being expanded to meet the large metal demands of the new tractor factory called Tractorstroi.

For Margaret, the tractor factory was the highlight of the Russian tour. The factory was an American-style operation supervised by American engineers. There Margaret satisfied her curiosity about the inexperienced Russian workers.

Margaret watched the workers and found them fascinated with the new technology, but not ready for the fast pace of the admired American assembly line. "One Russian is screwing in a tiny little bolt," wrote Margaret, "and twenty other Russians are standing around him watching, talking it over, smoking cigarettes, arguing."

As Margaret went through the factory, she searched for the most interesting faces, both young and old. Margaret found these people a joy to photograph. They were quick to understand her artistic efforts at composing a picture and did not become self-conscious as American workmen did.

Unlike her earlier Cleveland works, many of Margaret's Russian photos featured people. But although Margaret began placing more importance on people, she still saw them as "props" for the camera—something to be moved, posed, arranged and rearranged.

After weeks of eating canned beans, Margaret returned to Moscow with eight hundred photos and many hours of work still ahead of her. All eight hundred had to be developed for inspection by the Russian government before Margaret could take them out of the country. Finding a place for this work posed a problem.

Margaret toured Russia in 1930. While in Moscow, she photographed people standing on the steps of the State Grand Theatre.

Luckily, her interpreter, Lida Ivanovna, was clever. She approached the people of a small motion picture studio outside Moscow. "The American photo-correspondent has just a little work to do," she told them, "just a few films to develop. It will not take us very long."

The "little work" took thirty-six hours. When Margaret got to the point of rinsing the photos, she returned to her hotel room and worked nonstop, kneeling before a bathtub of cold water, while Lida fed her sandwiches.

The trip to Russia was important to Margaret for more than one reason. As a college student, Margaret had expressed an interest in writing. Now she had some memorable experiences for a major writing project. She took forty of the eight hundred photos and used them in *Eyes on Russia,* her first book, which was published in 1931.

When Margaret re-turned to Russia for her second visit, she focused on capturing the people's beauty in her pictures.

With a continuing interest in that country, Margaret re-turned to Russia that year at the invitation of the Soviet government. But this time she went with a different pho-tographic mission. Margaret took greater interest in the people. She looked more carefully at their faces and saw beauty there. She thought about the people and the work they did. In addition to recording her observations on film, once again Margaret chose to share her experiences with words. She wrote a series of six articles about Rus-sia for the *New York Times*. In "Silk Stockings in the Five-Year Plan," Margaret touched on the life of the new Russian woman, who was working the same jobs as men. In "Making Communists of Soviet Children," Margaret described how children were much loved in Russia and were looked upon as the cornerstone for the success of the Communist state.

During this second trip, Margaret found the Russians more comfortable and productive with their new machines. She found them capable, eager to learn, and willing to shift their efforts in new directions. In this way, they were like Margaret herself, for she was eager to learn and willing to take her work in new directions.

5

A Taste of Suffering

While Margaret was focusing on Russia's hopes for prosperity, America was falling off its carnival ride of productivity. By 1933 one of every four Americans was unemployed.

Being unemployed was not a concern for Margaret. During the Depression years, the assignments kept rolling in. In 1934 her fascination with flying began as she worked on an airline assignment to shoot the new Pan Am terminal in Miami. But though Margaret had plenty of work, she managed her finances poorly. The Bourke-White Studio brought in money, but her expenses were high. She had a staff to pay, and the Chrysler Building studio was expensive. Many of her clients, like many other Americans, had cash problems, and collecting fees was difficult. Eventually Margaret reached the point where she was borrowing money from her mother and everyone else she could.

In 1934, Margaret photographed the bleak, barren state of fields in the Dust Bowl.

But Margaret's financial troubles were small in comparison with those of many of the nation's people. In 1934 Margaret got her first real taste of human suffering on a grand scale. *Fortune* assigned her to take photos for "The Drought," an article about the suffering states in the Dust Bowl.

Margaret was given the assignment with only three hours to catch a flight west and not much information. Margaret knew only what others in the East knew. The fields in the Midwest—which had been overplowed and overgrazed by cattle for decades—had been stripped of topsoil. After years of severe drought conditions, the sun and relentless wind were now whipping what was left into a killing dust. Margaret wasn't even sure where the Dust Bowl was. After trying to get details from news sources, she flew to Omaha, Nebraska, to investigate the matter. As she soon learned, the Dust Bowl extended from the Texas panhandle to the Dakotas. Margaret had five days to cover the area in an old airplane.

Margaret was inexperienced in photographing people's suffering, but she attempted to show the hardships of pioneer families during the Depression.

Throughout these states, Margaret saw chicken coops and pigpens buried in dust. She heard of police getting calls from parents whose children were lost in the dust, and she learned of people dying in dust storms. As Margaret took her photographs, her assistant held the camera to the ground while wind lashed into her lens. When she was lucky, she snapped a quick shot before the lens became coated with sand.

Photographing these scenes was a new experience for Margaret. Human suffering was different from factories and machines. Margaret had not yet developed the understanding needed for this type of work. Her Dust Bowl photos were not the brilliant photos of the steel mills. Margaret saw the destruction caused by the dust storm—both to the land and the people. But her photographs did not capture the people's deep sadness or the hopelessness of the situation.

But what she didn't show on film, she expressed artfully in writing a year later, in her article "Dust Changes

America," published in the *Nation* magazine. "The dust storms have distinct personalities," she wrote, "rising in formation like rolling clouds, creeping up silently like formless fog, approaching violently like a tornado."

For her assignment, Margaret met ranchers and farmers. She saw the despair on their faces; she heard the hopelessness in their voices. "But the real tragedy," she wrote, "is the plight of the cattle. In a rising sand storm cattle quickly become blinded. They run around in circles until they fall and breathe so much dust they die."

The Dust Bowl experience left Margaret more unhappy than ever with the advertising business. She was beginning to develop concern for people and their problems, and this made it difficult to work in the commercial world, where selling a product was the only goal. Now Margaret wanted to do only honest, creative work. After having a nightmare about giant Buick cars chasing her, she decided to abandon her advertising accounts.

With a new desire to understand her fellow Americans, Margaret began thinking about different directions for her work. She began thinking in terms of a book project. But though Margaret enjoyed writing at times and was talented in this area, she considered herself a photographer, not a writer. So she looked for an author with similar ideas. She wanted someone who was concerned with social issues—with the lives and struggles of people—and who would accept having the photos play just as important a part in the book as the words.

The author who interested Margaret was Erskine Caldwell. Margaret arranged a meeting with him.

During her trip to the South in 1936, Margaret learned a great deal about people and was able to catch their spirit on film.

Erskine Caldwell was well known for his novels *God's Little Acre* and *Tobacco Road,* and he was planning to write a documentary work about the life of sharecroppers in the South.

Margaret did not know what to expect from Caldwell. He didn't talk much, and she had learned from his literary agent that he didn't like her advertising photos or the idea of working with a woman. But the meeting went well, and they decided to work together. They chose June 11, 1936 as a date to start the book.

After getting rid of her penthouse and finishing her advertising work, Margaret began the eight-state tour with Caldwell, traveling west from South Carolina and Florida to Louisiana. She took five cameras and a good supply of batteries to operate the flashbulbs for inside shots. (There was no electricity in many of the locations they visited.)

In the South, Margaret met poverty up close. Her pictures show rusting autos and sharecroppers' crumbling shacks, the inside walls covered with old newspapers, from floor to ceiling. They show the wrinkled faces of people weathered by despair. They show the poorly fed and the raggedly clothed.

During their house-to-house travels, Margaret heard how families could not send all their children to school in winter because there was not enough warm clothing to go around. She learned how the sharecropping system (in which farmers worked on land that they did not own) sucked the life out of the farmers, who would never be able to yield much of a profit from the worn-out soil. She listened to stories about the white plantation owners. They had divided their land into small one-family farms and were now landlords, collecting rent from the farmers without having to worry about the problems of working the land.

Margaret tried to keep in the background as she and Erskine traveled through the South. The people they wanted to interview and photograph didn't like strangers, especially Northerners. Erskine, Southern-born, was better at winning their trust. He knew the language and the ways of the people.

Margaret learned a great deal about people from him. She saw how Erskine waited patiently with a person—often not talking for long stretches of time—until the person was ready to "reveal his personality." Following Erskine's lead, Margaret set up a camera in the corner of the room. With a remote control in her hand, she remained silent, hoping for an expressive look to appear on her subject's face.

While working together, Margaret and Erskine became

friends. Erskine began calling Margaret "Kit," saying it suited her because she "had the contented expression of a kitten that has just swallowed a bowl of cream."

The friendship between them grew as they explored the back-country roads. So did the material for their book. One day they came across a chain gang (a group of prisoners chained together) working along the side of the road. It was something they had hoped to find. Margaret wanted a photograph of the men chained to each other, "each with his soup spoon tucked in his iron ankle cuff."

Getting the picture did not come easily. The surly captain of the gang wanted to know who gave them permission to take pictures, then bellowed some angry words and fired his gun at the wheels of their car. But Margaret and Erskine were not easily discouraged. They returned with a permit, and Margaret got her pictures.

Erskine Caldwell and Margaret Bourke-White

The months passed—eighteen months. In November 1937, their first book together, *You Have Seen Their Faces,* was published. Margaret was thrilled when she read the reviews. The *New Republic* gave the photos high praise, saying they were the dominant force while the text played a supporting role. And the comments by Harry Hansen of the *World-Telegram* left her inspired. He compared the pictures to portraits and applauded Margaret's ability to capture the innermost thoughts and spirit of the people. This was exactly what Margaret had set out to do. Her work with *Faces* was a professional leap as a photographer.

6

Life's "Picture Magic"

By the mid-1930s, Margaret no longer thought in terms of single pictures. She no longer thought as only a photographer. Now she thought as a journalist as well, though she still didn't consider herself a writer.

Margaret was now driven by social awareness—a concern for people and their living conditions—and her explosive talents needed a new outlet. Fortunately an opportunity emerged on the scene, exciting enough to challenge her fireball of ambition.

During the years when Margaret was developing her skills, photographic technology was racing forward alongside her. Among the advances, smaller cameras and wire services—news organizations that could send photographs anywhere—were changing the way news could be reported.

Henry Luce, the publishing giant who had hired Margaret for *Fortune*, recognized that it was time for photographs to play a more important role in magazines. With *Life*, a new magazine that Luce was planning to publish, Margaret's career and fame were about to leap to new heights.

In 1936, the busy, fast-paced American lifestyle presented a golden opportunity for Luce's genius. Leisure time was decreasing. Reading about the news was becoming a time-consuming chore for many people. Luce, with his fascination for what he called "picture magic," recognized that the time was ripe for a magazine devoted to pictures. Winning one of the most glamorous positions in the profession, Margaret began working for the new *Life* magazine, along with three other photographers: Alfred Eisenstaedt, Thomas D. McAvoy, and Peter Stackpole.

By this time, Margaret was known as an aggressive photographer who would stop at nothing to get her pictures and let nothing interfere with her work. Not many of her new colleagues at *Life* liked her. She kept to herself and didn't talk to people much. To some, it seemed she only smiled and was nice when she wanted a favor. One *Life* photographer asked Margaret if she would like to have lunch with her someday. Margaret replied that she was busy writing a book—she wouldn't be free to have lunch for several years!

In 1936, Margaret photographed workers on the Fort Peck Dam in New Deal, Montana.

Margaret's cold way with people did not stop the editors from appreciating her talent. For her first assignment, Margaret was sent to the huge Fort Peck Dam being built at New Deal, Montana. The editors expected that Margaret, with her industrial experience, would come up with some powerful construction pictures. Luce sent Margaret to this "lonely, primitive and wild" spot in northern Montana and told her to look for something impressively large that could be used for the cover.

Margaret knew what Luce wanted. Having the insight to recognize a photo opportunity came easily to her. Her picture of gigantic concrete piers towering over two people became the cover for the first issue.

But Margaret went beyond getting construction pictures. Driven by curiosity, she examined the dusty Montana settlement. She sent her editors a pictorial story of the wide-open shanty towns with their rickety shacks, tired-looking pioneer women, and beer bars. She sent them a compelling look at the ordinary people of these raw and unruly towns, with poor sanitation and little organized law enforcement.

When the editors saw Margaret's pictures, they were overwhelmed. They had not expected this powerful human interest story from Margaret. They had not expected Margaret to take them into the Wild West hot spots like the Bar X or Ruby's Place. It took their breath away to see a four-year-old girl sitting on a bar top, while her mother, a waitress, tended to her drinking customers. The bar looked like a rowdy spot—no place for a child. Margaret's photographs told the story of men out for a good time after a hard week at the construction site. It showed the men chugging down the liquor and dancing the night away with "taxi-dancers"—working ladies out to make a few bucks.

Luce was thrilled when he saw Margaret's pictures. He had been waiting for a good opening story for the magazine, and now he had it: "Whoopee at Fort Peck."

Margaret's pictures of men dancing with taxi-dancers impressed the editors at *Life*.

The first issue of *Life* magazine came out on November 23, 1936. Margaret's photo of Fort Peck Dam made a stunning cover.

The first issue of *Life* (at ten cents a copy) hit the newsstands on November 23, 1936. Margaret's cover of the dam and her picture story of Fort Peck nightlife served as a model for the magazine. Famous people would be scattered among the pages of *Life,* but candid shots of ordinary people would be the heartbeat of the magazine.

During this time before television was available, Margaret and the other *Life* photographers helped readers experience events in a way deeper than words could ever do. Readers felt the emotions of the people pictured— their joy, their surprise, their sorrow.

Working for *Life* was a dream come true for Margaret. She enjoyed the glamour and fame the job brought her. At times, the attractive and well-dressed Margaret even became the subject for other photographers. Margaret was given many of the photo essay assignments, and the editors began to refer to stories as a "Bourke-White" type of story, which gave her a great deal of satisfaction. She thrived on the fast pace of her work, the challenge of deadlines, and the travel into unfamiliar territory.

In January 1937, Louisville, Kentucky, took the spotlight as one of those unfamiliar territories when the Ohio River overflowed, flooding the town. *Life* sent Margaret racing to the airport with only one hour to catch a plane. She couldn't miss the flight. It wouldn't be long before the Louisville airfield was flooded and all flights were stopped.

Margaret caught the plane, but more problems awaited her in Louisville. With the highway under water, Margaret had to snatch rides in rowboats (and once in a raft) to reach the town.

With camera in hand, Margaret found the people side of the flooding story. The flooding waters had driven many families from their homes. Margaret saw suffering, kindness, and courage. She watched rescuers search for people who might be clinging to debris in the water or waiting for help on high ground. She watched people in rowboats bring food and bottles of clean drinking water to victims who were stranded.

Margaret's pictures in *Life* brought the tragedy of the flood into people's homes throughout the country.

Through photos like this one, Margaret let America know that poverty did, in fact, exist in the United States.

And it brought more. The first page of this lead story showed survivors standing in front of a billboard. The billboard picture displayed the smiling faces of a white family in a car, with the headline, "World's Highest Standard of Living. There's no way like the American Way." In front of the billboard were black men and women with unsmiling faces, lined up at a relief center, carrying pails, baskets, and bags. With that photo, Margaret brought a sad truth home to *Life* readers—the inequality and poverty that exist in this country.

During the early days of *Life,* most of the assignments dealt with life of the average American—families, sports, small-town activities. But the editors were not hesitant to send the staff on "extraordinary travel excursions." In 1937, for instance, *Life* sent Margaret chasing after the newly appointed governor-general of Canada, Lord Tweedsmuir, who was on a trip to the frozen reaches of his country in the Arctic Circle. At one point on the trip, Margaret set off with a pilot and two other men in an old seaplane. They flew north with the door of the plane removed. Margaret, with a rope tied around her waist, leaned out over the seas to take pictures.

In 1937, Margaret flew to the Arctic Circle to photograph Lord Tweedsmuir, the governor-general of Canada.

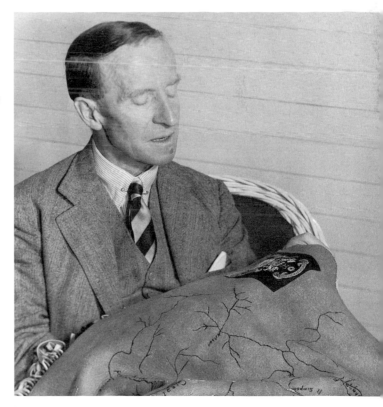

Before long, an Arctic fog rolled in, making flying impossible. With no landmarks to follow, Margaret's pilot guided the plane into sudden drops and rolls, searching for a spot to land, until finally he found a rocky island. But their troubles were not over. The radio was too weak to send a message for help, and they had no idea when the fog would lift. It looked like Margaret and the others might be stranded on the island for weeks with little food.

Luckily, "that evening, the fog cleared for an instant and the pilot raced them into the plane [and took off]." But this would not be Margaret's only brush with death. Many more would follow.

7

On the Edge of Death

In the 1940s, when World War II was raging in Europe, the country's attention shifted from problems at home to events overseas. Margaret's heart raced when she heard the trumpet call of war. She knew *Life* would hand her some exciting assignments.

In the spring of 1941, Margaret hurriedly packed for Russia at the request of Wilson Hicks, the picture editor at *Life*. Germany, led by their Nazi leader, Hitler, had invaded much of Europe. Hicks suspected that Russia would be the next country attacked. Margaret was eager to go, and so was her husband, Erskine Caldwell, whom she had married in 1939. Erskine's books were known in Russia.

Before they departed, Margaret had to plan her supplies carefully and learn how to make simple camera repairs.

Finding help in a war-torn country would not be easy. It took a month to assemble her luggage, which weighed six hundred pounds and held five cameras, twenty-two lenses and three thousand flashbulbs.

When Margaret and Erskine did leave, they traveled by way of China, since much of Europe was occupied by the Germans. They entered Russia on the southeastern side.

On June 22, just a month after they reached Russia, German troops stormed across the western border. It was a swift, thundering attack. More than a thousand Russian planes were destroyed. When news of the attack reached Margaret, she and Erskine left the small town they were visiting in the south and made a mad dash to Moscow to be closer to the action.

The day after they arrived at the National Hotel in Moscow, Margaret learned the Russian army had issued a ukase, an order banning the use of cameras. Anyone caught with a camera could be sent to prison or shot!

Wilson Hicks, the picture editor at *Life,* sent Margaret to Russia once again in 1941.

But Margaret was the only foreign photographer in Moscow. She was not going to miss this opportunity. She was skilled at getting her way, and after two weeks of daily phone calls and visits to important people, she got permission to take photographs. Now she had only to wait for German planes to approach.

While she waited, there were practice air-raid drills at night. When the sirens sounded, everyone, including Margaret and Erskine, was ordered to the shelters in the subway 100 feet underground. Margaret marveled at the subway stations; they were spotlessly clean. But she had no intention of hiding underground every night.

After missing the first night of actual bombing while waiting in a shelter, Margaret and her husband moved to the American Embassy building, where Russian rules did not apply. The second night, when they heard the hum of German planes on their way, they went up to the roof.

It was ten o'clock. Russian searchlights were scanning the black sky. Margaret watched the anxious lights searching for the German planes. She listened to the approaching low hum swell into a quake of deep rumbles overhead. What happened next, Margaret would never forget.

Margaret saw bursts of color and flashes of light that looked like fireworks. She saw German planes drop firebombs that exploded on the ground and sent flames shooting up to the sky. She watched Russian rockets streak upward and machine guns shoot back at the planes.

At a quarter after one, Erskine went to the radio station to send news of the attack to America, while Margaret stayed alone on the open roof. Standing there, on the edge of death, Margaret felt small and spellbound by the horror. She saw beauty in the heavenly show of destruction. She heard music in the killing sounds of the raid—the bombs whining as they fell, the boom and deeper echo of the guns.

Margaret stayed alone on the roof for some time with a strange sense of safety—as if her camera would protect her somehow. She pointed her camera toward the most dazzling action and, with each blast, hastily took shelter. But suddenly, Margaret had the feeling that something big was heading her way. In seconds, she grabbed the camera and climbed through the window.

Just as she dropped to the floor, a bomb exploded, shattering every window in the building. Margaret's fingertips were cut by the glass chips, but she was not badly injured.

The Germans bombed Moscow twenty-two times before Margaret left in September. She photographed the attacks almost every time. Her vivid pictures let Americans see what Germany was doing in Europe and may have helped push this country closer to war.

When Margaret returned to the States, the American public shared in her Russian war experiences, and not only from the pictures in *Life*. Some Americans were lucky to hear about the adventures from Margaret herself as she began a speaking tour of the United States.

While sorting out her experiences before her audiences (mostly women's clubs), Margaret entertained her listeners with details of her dangerous mission in Russia.

Although awestruck by the destruction around her, Margaret was able to take pictures of the horrifying—and sometimes beautiful—sights of the German raid on Russia.

Margaret was an exciting speaker, and she dazzled the audience with her glamorous wardrobe. Like an actress in costume, she dressed in a gold-brocade strapless gown for the evening, and Paris suits and hats decorated with birds' nests or witches' cones during the day.

Margaret also shared her war experiences by writing her second book about Russia, *Shooting the Russian War*. Margaret was a dynamic storyteller. Her skill at capturing life's drama on film spilled over into her writing. She became a master at spinning her adventures into a forceful, emotion-packed tale.

Professionally Margaret was having the time of her life, but her marriage was falling apart. Margaret's independence and devotion to work were difficult for Erskine to accept. Erskine's icy moods and withdrawal from Margaret put a strain on their relationship. After just a few years of marriage, they divorced in 1942.

8

Lessons in Courage

In the spring of 1942, Margaret traded her evening gowns and Paris suits for a uniform designed especially for her by the Army War College. She was appointed the first woman war photographer for the United States Army Air Forces and returned to Europe to work for both the military and *Life* magazine.

By this time, the United States had joined England, Russia, and the other countries fighting to stop Germany. In the summer, Margaret flew to England and joined the Air Force at a secret American base. There Margaret worked on a picture story about the thirteen B-17 bombers, known as the "Flying Fortresses," of the Ninety-seventh Bomb Group. She shot the crew's early morning meetings and went up in their "big lumbering airplanes" when they practiced.

Margaret was thrilled to be working for the Air Force.

She loved taking pictures from airplanes and begged to fly on combat missions. But the missions were dangerous, and even though the Air Force sent a few male reporters, they did not send Margaret.

Margaret was disappointed, but she soon learned of an opportunity for a different type of adventure. She heard about secret plans for a battle on the coast of North Africa. England and America were going to invade the coast and attack German forces there. This surely was an event Margaret did not want to miss. Her request to tag along was granted, and she was sent by sea while the bombers flew ahead.

The voyage, which was supposed to be perfectly safe, turned into a nightmare as soon as they steamed out of the harbor. The fleet of ships, carrying thousands of British and American troops and nurses, headed into a violent storm that lasted five full days.

Margaret was appointed the first woman war photographer for the U.S. Army Air Forces in 1942.

After they were res-
cued from lifeboats,
Margaret Bourke-White
and David Herbert
were able to relax.
Herbert helped to pick
up and treat survivors
from the water.

For Margaret, this voyage was a lesson in courage. She
did not get seasick, but most people became too sick to
eat, walk, sit up, or even talk. Margaret was awestruck
watching the sick nurses force themselves from their
bunks for daily lifeboat drills. And when the ship was
torpedoed by the enemy, she saw acts of bravery unlike
any she had experienced.

She saw nurses shaking uncontrollably with fear and
yet marching silently to their lifeboat stations as they had
been trained. She saw men scrambling down the rope
nets that hung from the side of the ship. She witnessed a

lifeboat full of nurses capsize into the sea. She herself was so terrified before her lifeboat was lowered that her mouth was dry with fear.

On that moonlit night, December 22, Margaret let thoughts of work banish her fears. She looked at the people swimming, the people hanging on to floating debris, and the sinking ship, and longed to use her camera. She imagined these scenes of disaster as photographs, and if it had not been so dark, they would have been. As it was, Margaret had to wait until sunrise. Then she photographed the people in her boat. Finally, after floating on the sea for eight hours, she and the others were rescued by another ship.

Margaret's brush with death did not lessen her desire to go on dangerous missions. When she landed in Africa, General Jimmy Doolittle, who had given her permission to come there, asked if she still wanted to fly on a combat mission.

"Oh, you know I do," Margaret gasped.

"Well, you've been torpedoed. You might as well go through everything," he said. Then he phoned the Ninety-seventh Bomb Group, and Margaret was flown to their secret air base in the Sahara Desert.

Margaret couldn't wait to fly with the bombers. She kept thinking about the target. Would it be an important one? Would she witness a major battle? Margaret hoped it would be one of the most important events of the war.

While Margaret waited, she prepared for the mission. Out in the desert heat, she dressed in heavy fleece-lined leather—jackets, leggings, and boots with lead weights.

Her flight would take her six miles upward into the air, and there the cabin would be an icebox. (Planes at that time were not heated.) Since bare flesh could freeze in an instant, Margaret was also given electric mittens. Once they were above 15,000 feet, she was told, she was never to remove them!

For two weeks, Margaret dragged her padded body and bulky camera through the crammed spaces of the plane. She crawled from window to window, searching for the best spots to take pictures.

Then, on the morning of the mission, Margaret gathered with hundreds of airmen among the ruined buildings of the village. It was January 22, 1943. The sky was cloudless. A cool wind was blowing. Margaret sat near a sand-swept fountain. She looked at the wall of covered maps and charts. The target was still a mystery.

Minutes before takeoff, the covers were removed from the maps and the mission was revealed. The El Aouina airfield in Tunis, Tunisia, was their target. Just what Margaret had hoped! This major target was a main air base where German troops were landing.

Margaret got the chance to christen a plane and name it Flying Flit Gun during World War II.

Margaret photographed Air Force pilots.

With no time to worry about her safety, Margaret boarded the lead plane, a B-17 loaded with bombs. There was no guarantee she would return alive. This was a mission of death—death for those on the ground and possibly for those in the air. But Margaret did not stop to think about this. When they lifted off, she began taking pictures of the men working in the plane.

As they neared the target, Margaret went to the bomb bay, where the bombs were stored. There, she squeezed herself and her bulky camera between the rows of bombs. Margaret looked at the bombs. Each had a safety pin, a device that prevented it from exploding too soon. Then she watched the crewman as he pulled out the pins. After a few minutes, she began taking pictures, without thinking about how nervous the crewman might feel pulling out the pins. She snapped a picture, and when the flash went off, the airman cried out in fright. He thought the bombs were exploding in his hands!

A short while later, Margaret's unit of planes joined another group, forming a force of thirty-two planes roaring toward the target. When they were directly overhead, the air attack began. The bomb-bay doors opened, and the bombs were dropped. Then the Germans shot back, and the planes tried to dodge their fire. Margaret's plane was hit twice in the wing. But Margaret kept taking pictures, not wanting to miss anything. After a battle in the sky between German fighter planes and the bombers, Margaret's plane escaped, and the German airfield was left ablaze.

During the bombing, Margaret did not think about all the people who were injured or killed on the ground. It was easy to forget them because she could not see them. But Margaret could not forget the wounded or dead when she was assigned to the ground forces in Italy. In a place called Purple Heart Valley, where American casualties were high, Margaret faced the human side of war.

Traveling in the war zone there was dangerous. The Germans had laid land mines, and Margaret learned how booby traps could be found in unexpected places. In buildings, explosives could be rigged in a doorknob, a chair, a floorboard, a piano, or a picture of Hitler. In the field, a bomb could be anywhere—in a bush or even on a dead body.

Margaret was warned about stepping off the road. The only safe spots were footprints or jeep tracks. With great care, she took photos of the American mine hunters, who had the nerve-racking job of sweeping the field for hidden explosives.

The risk in Purple Heart Valley was greater than any Margaret had faced before, and it was unpredictable. While traveling with the troops, Margaret found herself jumping out of her jeep at the sound of screaming whistles overhead and dashing for cover in muddy ditches. A flash of light announced the bursting shells, followed a second later by a roar. Then the explosions shook the ground and hurled spraying attacks of earth and rocks.

Traveling in the Purple Heart Valley in Italy, Margaret photographed some of the people—scared and distraught from the war—that she met along the way.

For Margaret, being in the ditches was more frightening than the bombing in Moscow. Here, she was trapped, in the middle of fire, with nowhere to hide. German shells swooshed overhead from one direction. American gunfire streaked from the other side.

Margaret tried to work and not think about death. But the steady rain often made her lenses and camera useless. She left the battlefront each day wondering about the soldiers. How could they stay in these mud holes for weeks without getting a break?

One day Margaret met a truckload of soldiers. They had been in battle for two months. She studied their tired, unshaven faces. Their bodies were alive, but they were dead inside. Some men would not be able to sleep or hear or function normally for some time.

In Italy, Margaret found that she no longer saw people as unfeeling props for her photos. She saw them as homesick and frightened soldiers, doctors, and nurses. For perhaps the first time, Margaret began listening to the people around her and learned that a camera can't catch everything. She realized how the honest and colorful conversation of the troops added depth to her stories. She learned to make observations not only as a photographer, but also as a writer.

Margaret's tour of the ground war also took her to the Eleventh Field Hospital, which was just a cluster of tents, each bearing a painted-on red cross. Margaret was still very close to the front line. The German forces were only six miles away, on a mountaintop. In fact, the night she arrived, a shell exploded only thirty feet from her tent and knocked out the camp's electricity.

The dining tent was completely destroyed, but the operating tent was still standing. So Margaret hurried there to watch the doctors and nurses work by the light of flashlights. Every time a shell whizzed toward them, the doctors and nurses dropped to the floor. Margaret marveled at how they routinely waited for the explosion, got up, checked the patients, and kept working.

Margaret stayed in the tent all night. As she took pictures, her heart went out to the wounded being carried in. She saw bodies ripped open and bleeding. She saw men with crushed legs and heard soldiers crying for the pain to stop.

Margaret was in the heart of the action when she toured Italy during the war.

The Army officers were glad that Margaret was taking pictures of the suffering and dying. They wanted the American people to know the truth about war. Margaret wanted the world to see the truth too. She wanted everyone to see how the nurses and doctors worked, hour after hour, in rain, wind, and constant danger. She stayed until she had her story.

When Margaret returned home and reached the *Life* office, she was greeted with some upsetting news. The hospital pictures that were sent to Washington, DC, had gotten lost somewhere in the Pentagon (where the U.S. Department of Defense is located). Margaret went wild when she heard this. She had risked her life for those pictures! In a rage, she flew to Washington and led a search of the shelves and files, hoping to find the pictures. She never did.

Angry and disappointed, Margaret took a break from the war zone. Over the next few months, she gathered her notes and wrote *They Called It "Purple Heart Valley."* With the conversations of troops, doctors, and nurses scattered throughout the book, Margaret created a memorable work.

In the spring of 1945, Margaret returned to Europe, this time to cover the biggest story of the war. She traveled with the U.S. Army, led by General Patton, as they swarmed into Germany, which by then was near defeat. As the troops entered the greater Frankfurt area, Margaret recorded the acts of chaos and violence that were breaking out among German soldiers and civilians. The night before their arrival, the Nazis had broadcast frightening statements to the German people, telling them they would receive savage treatment from the American soldiers. They ordered the people to leave and not to cooperate with the enemy. Then the Nazis set the food stores on fire and escaped from the city in cars.

Margaret witnessed the acts of a crazed people, some fleeing the city on foot, some walking in a daze carrying flowers. She photographed the bodies of a Nazi official and his family slumped over desks in his office—dead from a suicidal dose of poison.

In April Margaret followed Patton's troops into Buchenwald to free the prisoners held in the death camp there. Margaret, like the soldiers, had heard how for years, men, women, and children were herded into box-cars and sent to camps to be killed. She knew that many of these people were Jews—that Hitler hated the Jewish people, blamed them for the country's problems, and wanted them all dead.

But knowing all this did not prepare Margaret for what she saw on that sunny April day. When she and Patton's troops reached Buchenwald, they were shocked by what they found. There were bones and skulls in huge ovens. There were mounds of bodies—dead and naked. The people who were still alive looked like skeletons. Their heads were shaven, and they had barely enough flesh to cover their bones.

The grim sights were unbearable for Margaret, and she was thankful she had her camera. She needed something to put between herself, her eyes, and the ugly scene. She took pictures, but there was no rush of excitement or thrill.

At the concentration camp in Buchenwald, Germany, Margaret used her camera as a shield to put distance between herself and the shocking sights she encountered.

Margaret took pictures of dying men in their bunks. She took pictures of men standing silently behind a barbed wire fence. She forced herself to take these pictures so doubters would believe, and those who would care not to remember would never forget.

Buchenwald was only one of the death camps. There were many others. Millions of Jews, Gypsies, political opponents, and others had been murdered under Hitler's orders. Newsreels and magazines like *Life* brought these gruesome discoveries into homes around the world, shocking everyone who saw the truth. *Life* used Margaret's spring photos to tell the story of "Faceless Fritz."

The pictures Margaret took in Germany after the war showed complete destruction of the cities there.

That was what *Life* called the typical German, who represented the people who had started the war and had let the inhuman horrors occur.

After her work for *Life* was completed, Margaret stayed in Germany through October 1945. She had many questions she wanted answered. She thought about the evil and violence she had witnessed. She asked herself: Who were these Germans? Were Germans like Americans? Did they think the same way? How could the majority of people in a country let such hatred and evil rule their lives?

Margaret interviewed many people, some of them Nazis, and what they said frightened her. Most denied knowing anything about the camps. "We didn't know. We didn't know," Margaret kept hearing. Very few Germans wanted to accept the responsibility for the rise of Nazism or for the war. Some, after seeing pictures in the newspapers of concentration camps, even expressed displeasure with the released prisoners. They complained when the ex-prisoners asked to be served first in stores.

At times Margaret became angry and wanted to show her feelings and tell the Germans what she thought. But she knew she would gain more by listening. She saved her rage for her next book, *Dear Fatherland, Rest Quietly*, in which she described her German experiences.

9
Fears and Hopes

During the war years, Margaret had developed a genuine concern for human suffering. After the war, she still craved adventure and continued to compete for challenging assignments. But now she wanted to find adventures that would let her tell the stories of people's lives.

In the spring of 1946, *Life* sent Margaret to India, a British colony undergoing major political and cultural changes. India was soon to gain its independence from Britain, and its people were struggling with the issue of whether to stay one united country or become two nations, one primarily for those of the Hindu religion and one for Muslims.

From her experiences in Nazi Germany, Margaret had learned that changes in a country could mean changes for the entire world. She went to India planning to record the unfolding historical events in depth. Since covering the story meant meeting the leaders, top on Margaret's list was seeing Mohandas K. Gandhi (also called the Mahatma or Great Soul). This British-trained lawyer, who worked to improve the lives of his people, was a man who believed in change through peaceful means rather than violence. He was also publicly against industrialization and the use of machines. To see Gandhi, Margaret traveled into one of the poorest sections of India. There Margaret found Gandhi staying with India's lowest class of people, the "untouchables," and working at his *charka,* or spinning wheel.

When Margaret asked permission to photograph the tiny, bald, seventy-seven-year-old Gandhi, she was told she first had to learn to use the *charka* and understand the workings of the wheel. Though she had no interest in spinning, Margaret forced herself to take a lesson in order to get her photographs.

At the top of Margaret's list while in India was to take a photo of Mohandas K. Gandhi *(seen third from left).*

Margaret photographed Gandhi several times. Here *(seen fourth from right)*, Gandhi participates in a peace march.

While working the wheel, Margaret wondered why Gandhi was against machines. So many of his people were starving. Surely a tractor would help feed the hungry!

After that session, Margaret photographed Gandhi several other times. She also photographed the riots that soon erupted in the country. While Gandhi wanted a united India, Mohammed Ali Jinnah, a Muslim leader, wanted a separate nation for Muslims, to be called Pakistan. When Jinnah announced that if India was not divided it would be destroyed, violence erupted in the city of Calcutta.

Margaret raced to the bloody scene and photographed the slaughter for *Life,* but it was a difficult job. The streets were littered with the dead, some six thousand people and animals. This horrible event reminded her of Buchenwald, because of both the killing and the reason for the senseless murder—differences in religious beliefs and racial backgrounds.

During her two-year stay in India, Margaret also studied the caste system, which separated the people in terms of social position and determined the jobs they were allowed to hold. At one point, the assignment for *Life* took her into the leather tanneries where the "untouchables" worked. The tanneries, where cowhides were made into leather, were dangerous places.

When Margaret entered the tannery, her eyes began to tear from the fumes of the tanning pits, and she found it difficult to see. In the dim light, the brown bodies of young children moved up and down. Margaret learned they were standing in acid pits of lime and stamping on the cowhides. She learned that the acid caused bleeding and ate away at flesh. She learned how the children became deformed, and that there were no laws to protect them. Margaret took pictures to show the world.

In the swelling heat, Margaret took her camera into the worst streets of India, streets of great poverty and wretched smells. She saw people too weak to cry, squatting on the ground and scratching at weeds to eat. To Margaret these people looked like the helpless cattle of the Dust Bowl.

On her last day in India, she met with Gandhi one last time. Though there were differences between them, she was impressed by his faith in people. While he agonized over the violence and hatred in the world, Gandhi believed in the goodness of the human heart. But good did not triumph over evil that day. A few hours later, Gandhi was assassinated.

Learning of Gandhi's death, Margaret's first thought

was to get a photograph. She rushed to where Gandhi's body was laid out. The room was filled with grief-stricken people who had been close to Gandhi. Margaret sneaked in a camera and snapped a shot.

When the flash went off, the people became furious. Someone grabbed the camera and ripped out the film. Margaret was ushered out of the building and told to leave the grounds.

The people wanted to be left alone with their sorrow, but Margaret ignored their feelings. She *had* to get a photograph. She reloaded her camera, concealed it again, and tried to enter the building. She did not succeed.

When Margaret returned to her Connecticut home, she turned her experiences into yet another book. *Halfway to Freedom* told of the problems she found in India. But it also included hope—hope that the changing India, with its new laws, might help those suffering most.

Margaret had a harder time finding hope in South Africa, where *Life* sent her in 1950. Her assignment was to investigate and photograph this troubled nation. She entered a country where 8,500,000 black Africans were ruled by fewer than 2,500,000 whites.

At first Margaret was charmed by the breathtaking qualities of the veld, the treeless grasslands of the region, which she saw as a stage on which storms could rise and fall. But her impressions changed as she approached the city of Johannesburg. Along the road to the city, Margaret saw mounds of mine wastes and learned that this modern city of tall buildings and department stores was built on top of gold mines.

Margaret braved the danger of a mining cave wearing a crash helmet and carrying her camera.

Margaret went into the mining community to learn more. It was a Sunday, a day for weekly tribal dances, when Margaret stumbled across her first two subjects for the camera. They were native African men, gold miners, known as Numbers 1139 and 5122. Fascinated with the men, Margaret left the ceremony wanting to know more about them. After obtaining permission, she followed these men into the mines two days later.

The mine was deep underground, where there was a danger of cave-ins. With a crash helmet on her head and an emergency whistle dangling from her neck, Margaret descended two miles in a cage. At first, Margaret found conditions in the dark tunnels bearable. But soon the air felt hot and muggy. Then Margaret saw the two dancing miners she came to photograph. They were not the lively, graceful men she had remembered. Here below the earth, they were bare-chested workers with sad eyes and sweat streaming down their faces and tired bodies. The picture Margaret took of these men became one of her most telling and treasured photos.

Margaret could understand the weariness of these miners. For before long, she was seized by a severe fatigue, temporarily losing the use of her hands and her speech. As she was quickly taken to an open mine passage, she thought of the miners. How could they spend eleven hours a day underground, when she had been there for only four? How could they bear the hard work, long hours, and low pay of the mines? She knew that the miners had no real choice.

Margaret's photograph of two native South African gold miners became one of her most treasured.

The longer Margaret stayed in South Africa, the angrier she became. She wanted to speak out against the wrong-doing she found. She did not want to lie in order to do her work. But Margaret needed the white official's help if she was to complete her assignment.

During her travels, Margaret met white citizens who were as outraged as she, but they were few. Most of the whites believed that they were better than the nonwhite South Africans. They wanted the blacks to remain un-skilled and ignorant. It hurt Margaret to see this. Espe-cially since it reminded her of the experiences she had had in the American Deep South, where the "Negro" was considered lazy and not as bright as the white person.

The prejudice in South Africa was intense. Nonwhite South Africans were forced to carry passes to travel from one area to another, and police often broke into homes searching for the residents' passes. Margaret went with the police on one such raid and watched them charge through a shantytown (a group of small, simple houses where many black South Africans lived) with clubs and guns. Margaret never forgot the look of terror on the children's faces as the police tore through their village.

The only glint of hope Margaret saw in South Africa was the few black miners who had been taught by mis-sionaries. They were trying to pass along their knowl-edge of reading, writing, and arithmetic during their trickle of free time.

Wherever Margaret went in the world, she searched for the stories of ordinary people struggling with the unfold-ing drama of their lives. On June 25, 1950, Communists from North Korea invaded South Korea, in what became known as the Korean War. After war had been raging for two years, Margaret asked *Life* to send her on an assignment in Korea.

Although several of her *Life* colleagues had done an outstanding job reporting the events of the war, Margaret felt that the most important aspect of the story, the Korean people, had not been covered. Margaret did not know how the specifics of the story would develop, but she went to Korea in 1952, eager to begin the detective work.

A glimmer of an idea surfaced when she heard about Communist guerrilla warfare. Early in the Korean War, Margaret learned, the Communists had managed to convert some of the youth over to their way of thinking. And now, these youth were organized into stealthy, fast-acting fighting forces known as guerrillas. They were stealing from the peasants and setting fire to the villages.

As Margaret gathered information, the hint of an idea took the shape of a story. She planned to take her camera into the lives of families torn apart by the Communists. But how she would get her pictures was still a mystery. And doing it without getting killed was another matter. The general rules of war (known as the Geneva Conventions) stated that war correspondents could be captured but not killed, but Margaret wasn't sure the Communist guerrillas would abide by those rules. Nevertheless, Margaret searched the countryside with the help of the South Korean police and the courageous Korean people.

Before long, the group found a band of guerrillas, whom the police quickly arrested. When Margaret saw the terrorists, she was shocked. They were only high school age children.

Why had these children joined the Communists? They were so young to be carrying guns. Margaret needed this question answered. Every time the police captured a band of guerrillas, she interviewed the youths. One young woman told Margaret the Communists promised to teach them to read and write and to provide them with a better life.

Slowly, the story began coming together. But a piece was still missing. That is, until Margaret met Nim Churl-Jin. Churl-Jin had been a guerrilla until he saw Communist soldiers beat the villagers, steal their food, and burn their houses. Now he wanted to return home.

When Margaret heard his story, an image of his homecoming flashed before her eyes. With police consent and with the help of a guide, Captain Pak, she arranged a jeep ride home for Churl-Jin. Two days later, Margaret recorded the emotional reunion in a rice field—Churl-Jin embraced by his mother.

Margaret traveled to South Korea, where she met Churl-Jin and his mother.

From the Korean war fields, Margaret stepped onto a more peaceful stage. During the winter of 1953-54, she entered the world of the Catholic Jesuits. Her photographs of Jesuit activity and training for the priesthood were used in a photo essay for *Life* in October of 1954, and in 1956 in the book *A Report on the American Jesuits* written by Father John LaFarge, S.J.

Unfortunately, vigor and work were beginning to slip from Margaret at this point. For two years, she had been experiencing the early symptoms of Parkinson's disease, which would be the last challenge of her life.

Afterword

For almost twenty years, Margaret fought a battle with Parkinson's disease, an illness of the nervous system that slowly robbed her of movement and speech. She endured two brain operations and the constant struggle of daily exercise to keep the use of her arms, fingers, and legs.

Retaining her courage, Margaret found strength from watching others. While forcing her fingers to type during a physical therapy session, she was inspired by the man across from her. He was tapping out the letters with a stick in his mouth. (He was unable to reach the keys because he was born with abnormally short arms.)

In her home in Connecticut, Margaret did exercises for her hands, such as making balls out of newspaper, as part of her Parkinson's disease therapy.

Margaret continued to take pictures until late in life, when Parkinson's disease made her unable to handle her camera.

During her last years, when she could no longer handle the camera, Margaret wrote her autobiography, *Portrait of Myself.* She was not surrounded by family or friends. For Margaret did not have many friends. Work had been her life, and she did whatever it took to get her pictures with little regard for people's feelings. If she thought female charm would work, she used it. If barking orders and using a harsh approach seemed necessary, she resorted to that. Some fellow photographers thought Margaret was too aggressive. At times, she may have been. But she used her talents, she did her best, and she shared her discoveries with the world.

On August 27, 1971, Margaret Bourke-White died at Stamford Hospital in Connecticut. She will be remembered for different reasons by many people.

Throughout her life, Margaret had raced with the dream of living a glamorous and exciting life. But while the camera gave her the chance for exploration and thrills, it also forced her to face the suffering, evil, and ugliness in the world.

But no matter what Margaret saw, she never lost her childlike enthusiasm for life. She thought the world was wonderful. And she thought that if people saw the truth, remembered it, and worked to make things better, life could be a thrilling adventure for everyone.

Notes

Page 8
Joseph was a follower of a movement known as Ethical Culture and introduced Minnie to this way of thinking. Followers of Ethical Culture believe in helping others through social change, but they do not necessarily believe in God.

Page 50
After the Civil War, whites and blacks in the South were able to farm under a system known as sharecropping. The white or black farmer rented land from a landlord and worked the land for a share of the crop and the income. The landlord gave the farmer a place to live and paid for supplies.

Page 63
In the spring of 1940, Margaret quit her job with *Life* to work for a new magazine called *PM*. Margaret felt that at times *Life* wasn't using her talents to the fullest. She thought *PM* magazine would offer her greater opportunities. But it didn't, and Margaret left *PM* in the fall of 1940 and returned to *Life*.

Page 63

Many photographers were jealous of the fact that Margaret got such important assignments. Some accused *Life* of giving her the best stories. In 1940 one staff member reportedly resigned from the magazine because of this.

Page 84

In 1947, India officially became independent. At the same time, it was divided into two countries, India and Pakistan. Pakistan was established as a Muslim state. A part of northeastern India became East Pakistan, and northwestern portions of India became West Pakistan. Hindus and Muslims clashed in riots in both countries. Millions of Muslims fled to Pakistan, and Hindus and members of other ethnic groups living in the new nation fled to India. In the 1970s, East Pakistan became a new, separate nation, Bangladesh.

Page 94

Margaret's mother died in 1936, and her sister died in 1965. During the years in which Margaret struggled with Parkinson's, her brother lived in Chicago, far from her home in Connecticut.

Bibliography

Books About Margaret Bourke-White:

Callahan, Sean, editor. *The Photographs of Margaret Bourke-White.* Greenwich, Connecticut: New York Graphic Society, 1972.

Goldberg, Vicki. *Margaret Bourke-White: A Biography.* New York: Harper & Row, Publishers, 1986.

Silverman, Jonathan. *For the World to See. The Life of Margaret Bourke-White.* New York: Viking Press, 1983.

Tucker, Anne, editor. *The Woman's Eye.* New York: Alfred A. Knopf, 1973.

Books By Margaret Bourke-White:

"Dear Fatherland, Rest Quietly." New York: Simon and Schuster, 1946.

Eyes on Russia. New York: Simon and Schuster, 1931.

Halfway to Freedom. New York: Simon and Schuster, 1949.

Portrait of Myself. New York: Simon and Schuster, 1963.

Shooting the Russian War. New York: Simon and Schuster, 1942.

The Taste of War. (Introduced and edited by Jonathan Silverman.) Great Britain: Century Publishing Co., Ltd., 1985.

They Called It "Purple Heart Valley." New York: Simon and Schuster, 1944.

You Have Seen Their Faces, by Erskine Caldwell and Margaret Bourke-White. New York: Arno Press, 1975.

Articles About Margaret Bourke-White:

Canavor, Natalie. "Margaret Bourke-White: a retrospective." *Popular Photography,* 72 (May 1973).

Cousins, Norman. "Obituary of Margaret Bourke-White." *Saturday Review,* 54 (September 11, 1971).

Deschin, Jacob. "She Held a Mirror to the World." *Popular Photography,* 70 (January 1972).

Mydans, Carl. "Unforgettable Margaret Bourke-White." *Reader's Digest,* 101 (August 1972).

Nall, T. Otto. "The Camera is a Candid Machine: An Interview with Margaret Bourke-White." *Scholastic,* 30 (May 15, 1937).

Articles By Margaret Bourke-White:

"The Best Advice I Ever Had." *Reader's Digest,* 70 (May 1957).

"Dust Changes America." *Nation,* 140, (May 22, 1935).

"Famous Lady's Indomitable Fight." *Life* (June 22, 1959).

"My First Job." *Ladies Home Journal,* 74 (April 1957).

"Making Communists of Soviet Children." *The New York Times Magazine* (March 6, 1932).

"Photographing This World." *Nation,* 142, (February 19, 1936).

"Silk Stockings in the Five-Year Plan." *The New York Times Magazine* (February 14, 1932).

Additional Sources:

LaFarge, John. *A Report on the American Jesuits.* (Photography and Note by Margaret Bourke-White). New York: Farrar, Straus and Cudahy, 1956.

Scherman, David E., editor. *The Best of Life.* New York: Time-Life Books, 1973.

Wainwright, Loudon. "Life Begins: The birth of the late great picture magazine." *Atlantic Monthly,* 241 (May 1978).

Index

Acknowledgments

Photographs are reproduced through the courtesy of: © AP/Wide World Photos, front and back
cover, pp. 71, 98; the Estate of Margaret Bourke-White, pp. 2, 10, 11, 13, 14, 19, 20, 22, 25,
29, 31, 38, 41, 44, 50, 73; © Fred Peel, 6; UPI/Corbis-Bettmann, p. 17; National Archives, pp.
28 (66-M-43-2), 43 (131-WP-91-4), 70 (208-PU-221S-3); Margaret Bourke-White/*Life* Magazine © Time Inc., pp. 33, 56, 57, 58, 60, 61, 67, 76, 78, 81, 82, 85, 86, 89, 90, 93; © Time,
Inc., p. 36; Margaret Bourke-White/*Fortune* Magazine/© Time, Inc., 37, 47, 48; Corbis-
Bettmann, p. 39; UPI/Bettmann, pp. 52, 74; Carl Mydans/*Life* Magazine © Time Inc., p. 64;
© Stuart Abbey, 96 (top); Alfred Eisenstaedt/*Life* Magazine/© Time, Inc., 96 (bottom).